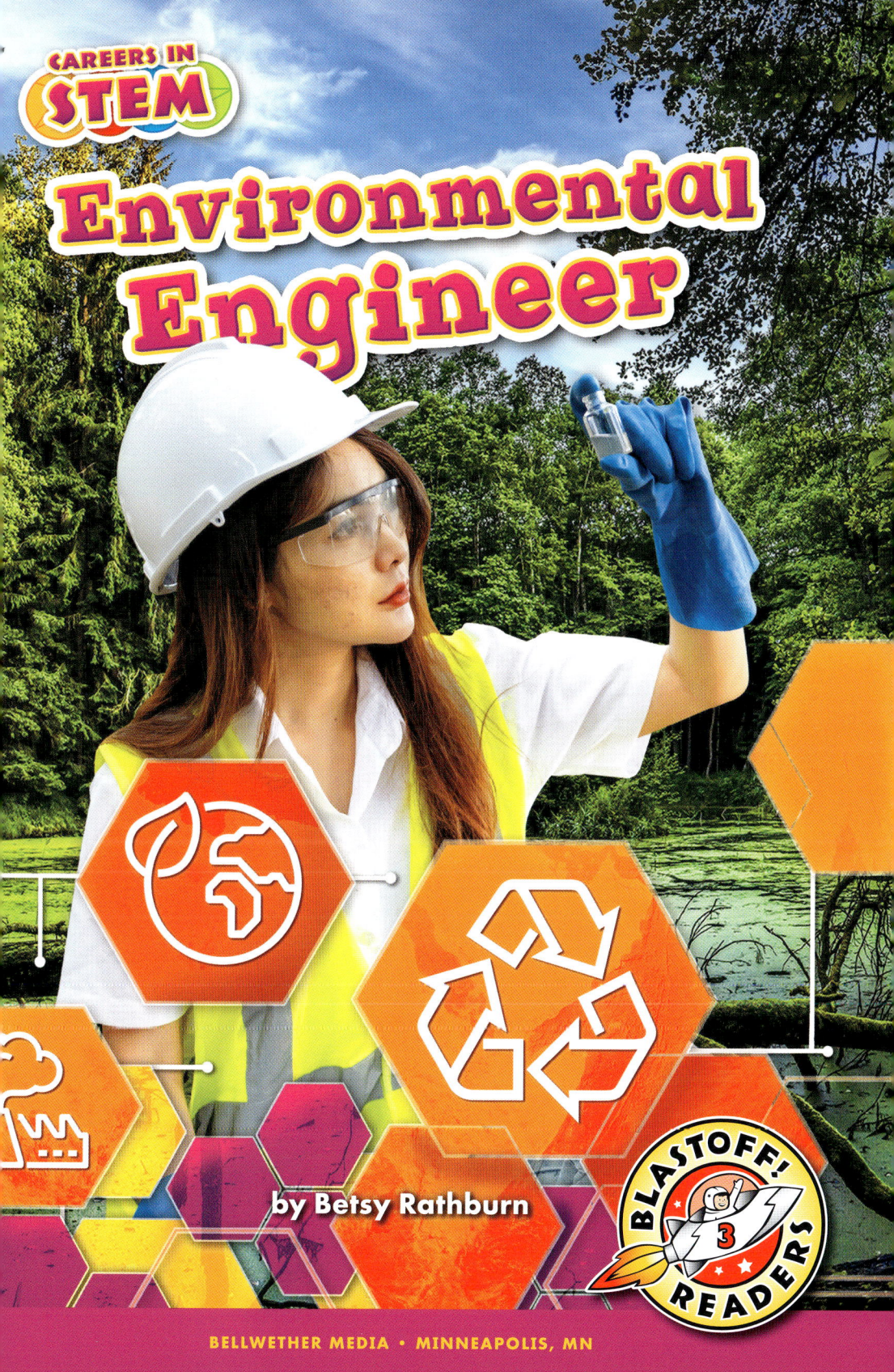

Blastoff! Readers are carefully developed by literacy experts to build reading stamina and move students toward fluency by combining standards-based content with developmentally appropriate text.

Level 1 provides the most support through repetition of high-frequency words, light text, predictable sentence patterns, and strong visual support.

Level 2 offers early readers a bit more challenge through varied sentences, increased text load, and text-supportive special features.

Level 3 advances early-fluent readers toward fluency through increased text load, less reliance on photos, advancing concepts, longer sentences, and more complex special features.

★ **Blastoff! Universe**

Reading Level

Grade K

Grades 1–3

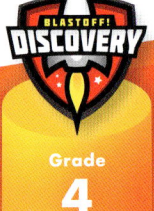
Grade 4

This edition first published in 2023 by Bellwether Media, Inc.

No part of this publication may be reproduced in whole or in part without written permission of the publisher. For information regarding permission, write to Bellwether Media, Inc., Attention: Permissions Department, 6012 Blue Circle Drive, Minnetonka, MN 55343.

Library of Congress Cataloging-in-Publication Data

LC record for Environmental Engineer available at: https://lccn.loc.gov/2022036401

Text copyright © 2023 by Bellwether Media, Inc. BLASTOFF! READERS and associated logos are trademarks and/or registered trademarks of Bellwether Media, Inc.

Editor: Elizabeth Neuenfeldt   Designer: Andrea Schneider

Printed in the United States of America, North Mankato, MN.

Table of Contents

Testing the Waters	4
What Is an Environmental Engineer?	6
At Work	10
Becoming an Environmental Engineer	18
Glossary	22
To Learn More	23
Index	24

Testing the Waters

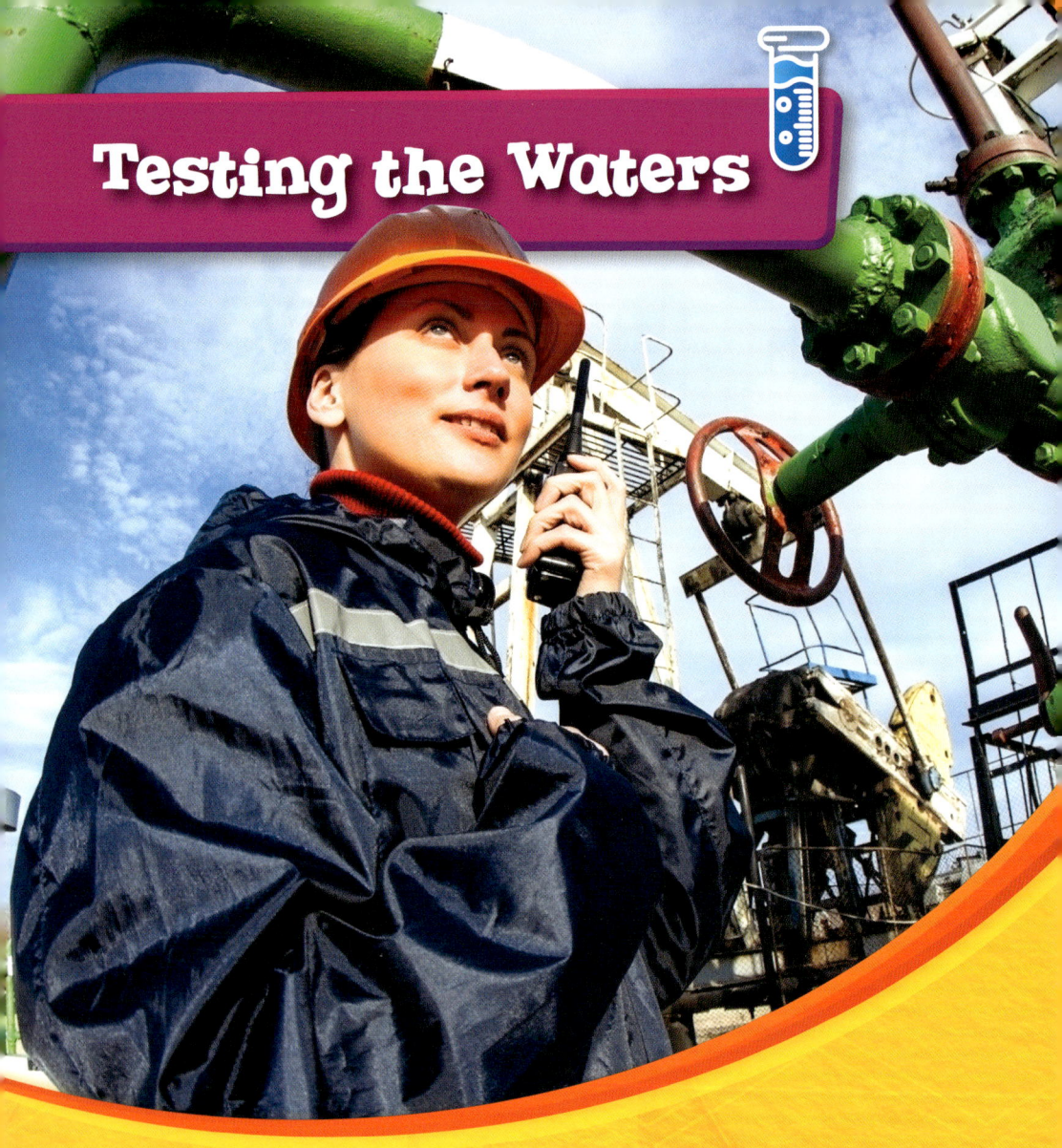

An environmental engineer visits an **oil field**. She takes dirt and water **samples**.

Later, she tests the samples in a **lab**. She makes sure the oil field is safe for people!

samples

oil field

What Is an Environmental Engineer?

Environmental engineers work to keep the **environment** safe. They find new ways to **recycle**.

They work to control **pollution**. They try to make water safe to drink. They work to clean the air and dirt.

recycling

Some engineers work outside. They visit places to check the environment. Others work in offices.

Engineers may work for businesses or governments. Their work keeps Earth clean!

Famous Environmental Engineer

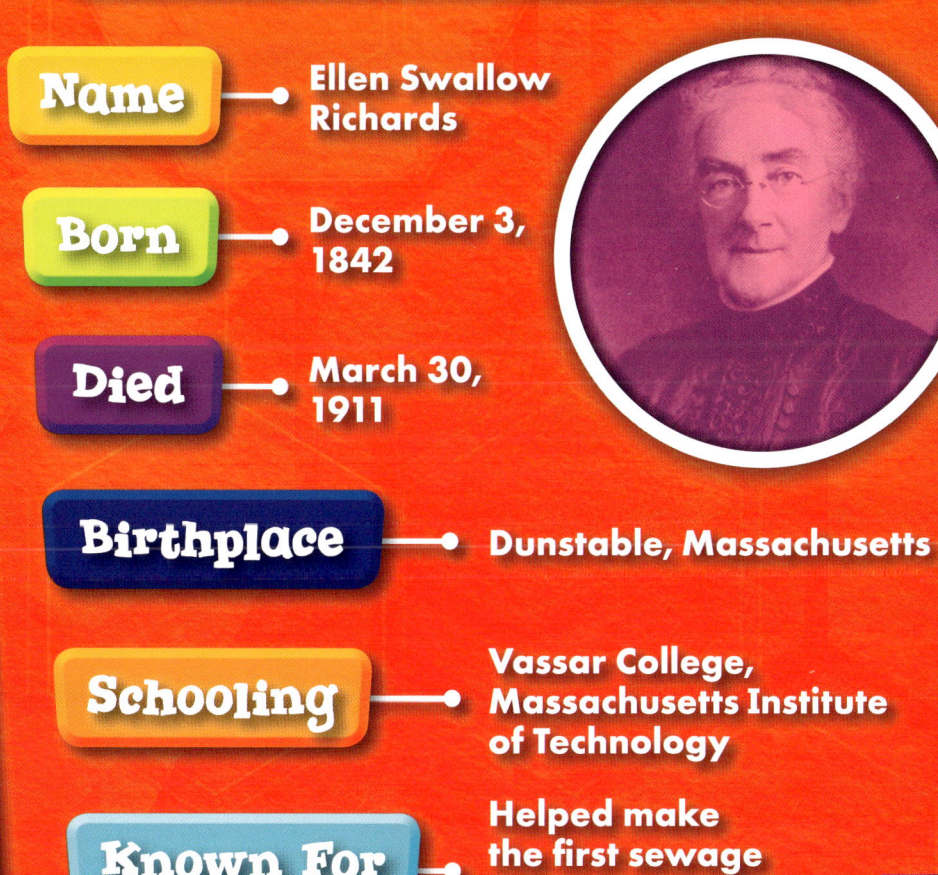

Name: Ellen Swallow Richards

Born: December 3, 1842

Died: March 30, 1911

Birthplace: Dunstable, Massachusetts

Schooling: Vassar College, Massachusetts Institute of Technology

Known For: Helped make the first sewage treatment plant in the United States

At Work

Environmental engineers take samples. They test dirt and water in labs.

They look for harmful **chemicals**. These can make plants unsafe to eat. They can make people and animals sick.

lab

tool used to measure pollution levels

They help control pollution. They use tools to measure pollution levels. They record and study the numbers they find.

They use the information to create **treatment systems**. These keep water clean.

treatment system

Some environmental engineers work in unsafe areas. They may visit oil or **sewage** spills.

Using STEM

Science — study the effects of chemicals

Technology — use tools to measure pollution

Engineering — make new ways to recycle

Math — use graphs to study changes

oil spill

They study the harm caused by the spills. They find ways to stop future spills.

low water levels due to climate change

Some engineers work with lawmakers. They help make laws that fight **climate change**.

These laws help keep plants and animals safe. They also help people live healthier lives!

Environmental Engineering in Real Life

clean drinking water

good dirt for growing food

trash and recycling programs

Becoming an Environmental Engineer

Environmental engineers go to college. They study math and science. They learn in labs. They take computer classes, too.

Many get **internships**. They learn from **experts**.

expert

science lab

Some engineers go to **graduate school**. They choose a subject to study further.

How to Become an Environmental Engineer

1. study math and science in college
2. get an internship
3. go to graduate school
4. find a job

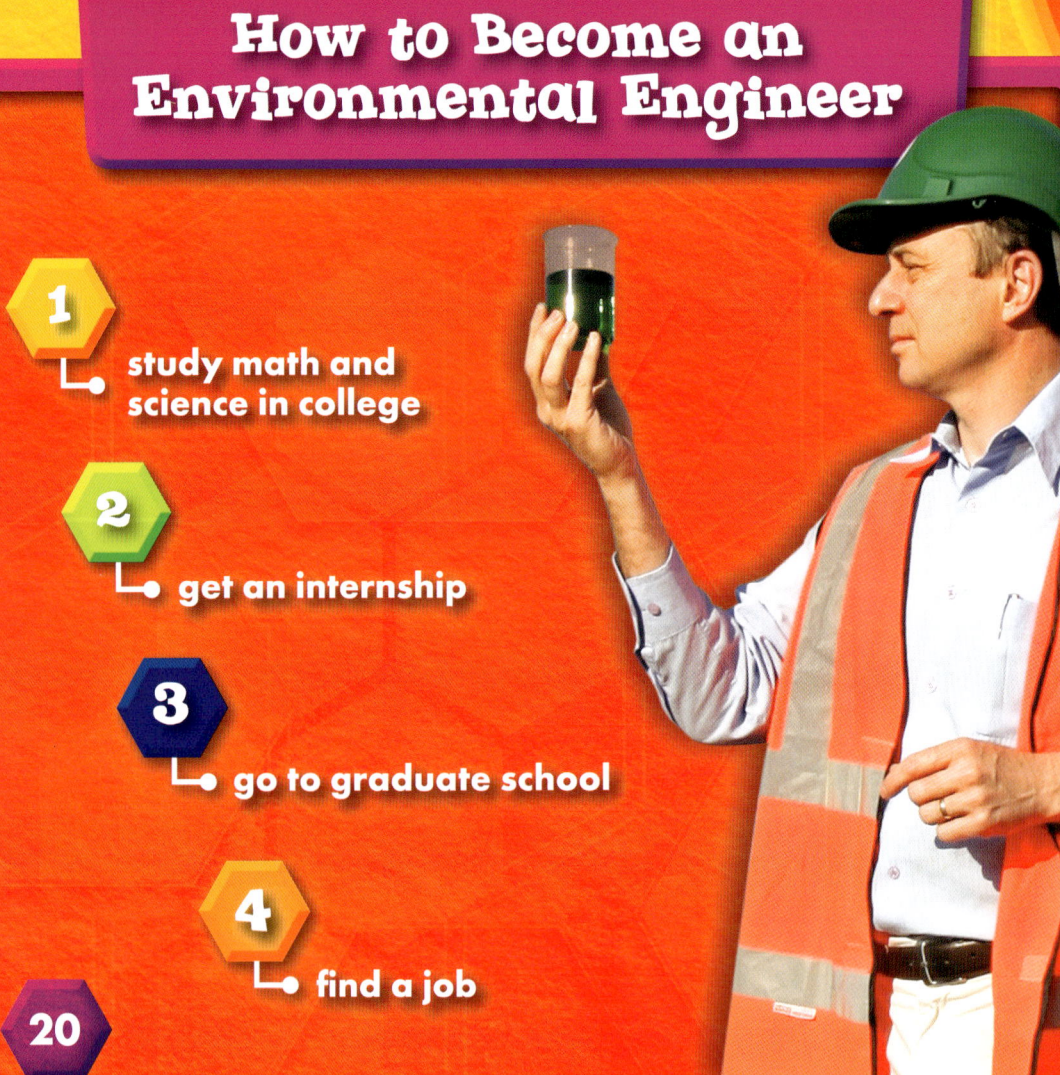

Then, they get jobs. These engineers help keep our planet clean and healthy!

Glossary

chemicals—materials that can cause a change in other materials

climate change—a human-caused change in Earth's weather due to warming temperatures

environment—the natural world

experts—people who have a lot of knowledge or experience in a certain area

graduate school—a school where people can study a specialty area after college

internships—programs where people work at a job to gain work experience

lab—a building with special tools to do science experiments and tests

oil field—an area of land or water where a lot of oil is found

pollution—substances that make air, water, or land dirty and not safe to use

recycle—to make something used into something new

samples—small amounts of things that give information about where they were taken from

sewage—waste water

treatment systems—processes that turn dirty water into clean water that can be used

To Learn More

AT THE LIBRARY

Bailey, R.J. *Environmental Engineer.* Minneapolis, Minn.: Jump!, 2019.

Knutson, Julie. *Flint Water Crisis*. Ann Arbor, Mich.: Cherry Lake Publishing, 2021.

Leaf, Christina. *Rachel Carson: Environmentalist*. Minneapolis, Minn.: Bellwether Media, 2019.

ON THE WEB

FACTSURFER

Factsurfer.com gives you a safe, fun way to find more information.

1. Go to www.factsurfer.com.
2. Enter "environmental engineer" into the search box and click.
3. Select your book cover to see a list of related content.

Index

air, 6
animals, 10, 17
businesses, 9
chemicals, 10
climate change, 16
college, 18
computer, 18
dirt, 4, 6, 10
Earth, 9
environment, 6, 8
environmental engineering in real life, 17
experts, 18
governments, 9
graduate school, 20
how to become, 20
internships, 18
lab, 5, 10, 18, 19
laws, 16, 17
math, 18
offices, 8
oil field, 4, 5
people, 5, 10, 17

plants, 10, 17
pollution, 6, 7, 12
recycle, 6
Richards, Ellen Swallow, 9
safe, 5, 6, 17
samples, 4, 5, 10
science, 18, 19
spills, 14, 15
study, 12, 15, 18, 20
tests, 5
tools, 12
treatment systems, 13
unsafe, 10, 14
using STEM, 14
water, 4, 6, 10, 13

The images in this book are reproduced through the courtesy of: kittirat roekburi, front cover (environmental engineer), p. 13; Apolinariy, front cover (background); robert_s, p. 3; ded pixto, pp. 4-5; serato, p. 5 (samples); qingqing, p. 5 (oil field); S.SUPHON, p. 6 (recycling); Corepics Vof, pp. 6-7; PONG HANDSOME, pp. 8-9; Wiki Commons/ Wiki Commons, p. 9 (Ellen Swallow Richards); Hero Images Inc./ Alamy, p. 10 (lab); Tan Kian Yong, pp. 10-11; Simon Turner/ Alamy, pp. 12-13; Phonix_a, pp. 14-15; Vadim Startsev, pp. 16-17; Riccardo Mayer, p. 17 (clean drinking water); Joanne Dale, p. 17 (good dirt for growing food); Tong_stocker, p. 17 (trash and recycling programs); goodluz, p. 18 (expert); wavebreakmedia, pp. 18-19; Keith Frith, p. 20 (environmental engineer); JohnnyGreig, pp. 20-21; tanuha2001, p. 23.